Arts and Crafts Fun

# Fun Crafts with
# Shapes

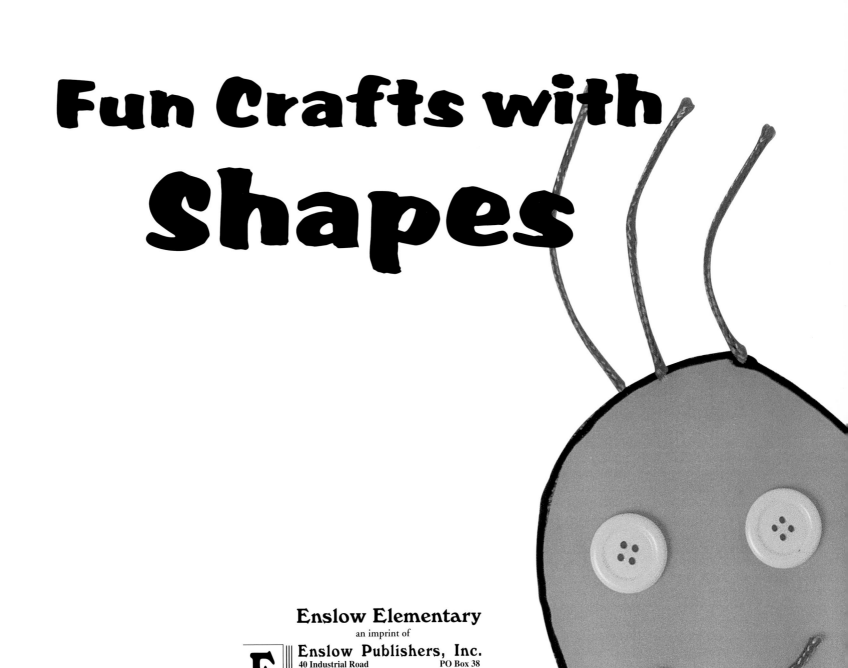

**Enslow Elementary**
an imprint of
**Enslow Publishers, Inc.**

E

40 Industrial Road      PO Box 38
Box 398      Aldershot
Berkeley Heights, NJ 07922    Hants GU12 6BP
USA      UK
http://www.enslow.com

Enslow Elementary, an imprint of Enslow Publishers, Inc.

Enslow Elementary® is a registered trademark of Enslow Publishers, Inc.

Translated from the Spanish edition by Toby S. McLellan, edited by Susana C. Schultz, of Strictly Spanish, LLC.  Edited and produced by Enslow Publishers, Inc.

**Library-in-Cataloging Publication Data**

Ros, Jordina.
  [Formas. English]
  Fun crafts with shapes / Jordina Ros, Pere Estadella.
      p. cm. — (Arts and crafts fun)
  Originally published: Barcelona, Spain : Parramón, c2004.
  ISBN 0-7660-2657-4
  1.  Art—Technique—Juvenile literature. 2.  Shapes—Juvenile literature. 3. Handicraft—Juvenile literature.  I. Estadella, Pere. II. Title. III. Series.
  N7440.R67613 2005
  701'.8—dc22
                              2005011222

Originally published in Spanish under the title *Las formas.*
Copyright © 2004  PARRAMÓN EDICIONES, S.A., - World Rights.
Published by Parramón Ediciones, S.A., Barcelona, Spain.
Spanish edition produced by:   Parramón Ediciones, S.A.
Authors:   Jordina Ros and Pere Estadella
Collection and scale model design: Comando gráfico, S.L.
Photography: Estudio Nos & Soto Corel, Corbis. Sculpture photo: © Successió Miró, 2003.
Parramón Ediciones, S.A., would like to give special thanks to Pol, Irene, and Carlota who did such a wonderful job posing for the photographs in this book.

Printed in Spain

10 9 8 7 6 5 4 3 2 1

# Fun Crafts with
# Shapes

# Table of Contents

# Things to Remember...

**Make sure you have everything you need!**
Before you start the craft, go over the list
of materials.

**Be careful with sharp objects!**
You may be using sharp tools, such as scissors
or something to punch holes with. Always ask
an adult for permission or for help.

**Working with clay**
Before beginning a craft that uses clay, protect
your workspace with newspaper or wax paper.
Keep your clay moist by wrapping it in a moist
cloth when you are not using it.

**Imagination**
If you come up with a new idea while working
on these crafts, tell a teacher or another adult.
Together you can create new crafts that are all
your own.

# What Is a Shape?

Shape has to do with how something looks on the outside—
the kind of form it has around its edges. Is it round? Square?
Irregular? Shape is recognized by sight or by touch.

*A shape can be open or closed, filled-in or empty, symmetrical
(the same on both sides if you cut it in half) or asymmetrical, and more.*

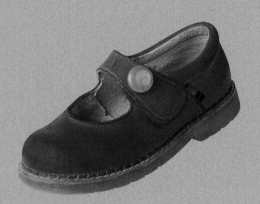

Open Shape

Closed Shape

Closed, Empty Shape

2D Shape          3D Shape

A shape may be on a flat surface (two-dimensional, or 2D)
or it may have volume (three-dimensional, or 3D).

Anything you can see has a shape. You can also make your
own shapes.

# Looking at Shapes

*Do you want to make shapes?*
*It's very easy!*

*Cover a chair with a sheet.*
*Now it has a different shape!*

How can you tell different shapes apart? Look at some objects. What size are they? What do they look like around their edges? Are their surfaces even and smooth, or uneven and rough?

Two objects may have different sizes and surface textures, but still have the same basic shape. The CD is bigger and has a smoother surface than the button, but they are both round. They may have similar sizes and surface textures, but different shapes. The two rocks are about the same size, and both have rough surfaces, but their outlines show that they have different shapes.

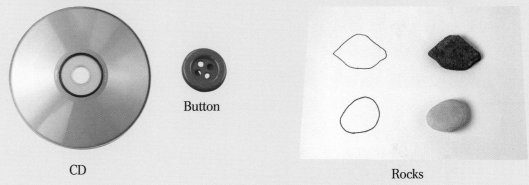

CD    Button    Rocks

Divide a shape down the middle. If the two parts you end up with are the same, the shape is symmetrical. If they are different, the shape is asymmetrical.

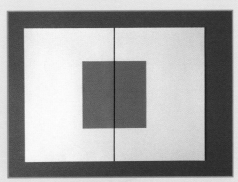

*A square is symmetrical!*

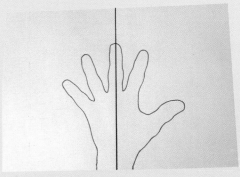

*A hand is asymmetrical!*

# Types of Shapes

## Geometric shapes

The first geometric shapes that most people recognize are the circle, the square, and the triangle.

## The two-dimensional (2D) or flat shape

A two-dimensional shape is flat. It has two dimensions—width and height.

*If you draw the outline of an object, such as a toy car, you will get a flat or 2D shape.*

## The three-dimensional (3D) or raised shape

A three-dimensional shape has volume. It has three dimensions—width, height, and depth.

*A sheet of newspaper is a 2D shape. If you crumpled it into a ball, you would have a 3D shape!*

# Shapes All Around Us

The clouds, the sea, mountains, fields, and sand… all of them have different shapes. In autumn, trees lose their leaves. Their shapes are very different than when their branches are full.

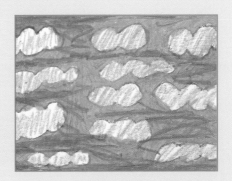

*Look at the sky! Can you draw the shapes of the clouds?*

The same shapes are repeated again and again in these tiles.

*The moon changes shape every night!*

The buildings in this city have many different shapes.

*We are surrounded by shapes! Just look around…*

# *Geometric Shapes*

## What you will need...

Black poster board
Green, orange, and blue clay
Square, round, and triangular stickers (different colors)

*How would you like to make the three basic geometric shapes?*

Mold three sticks of green clay, one of orange clay, and four of blue clay.

Place the three green sticks on the black poster board in the shape of a triangle.

Make a circle with the orange stick. Make a square with the four blue sticks.

*Fill each shape with matching stickers!*

Put different colored triangular stickers inside the green clay triangle, circular stickers inside the orange circle, and square stickers inside the blue square.

*The three basic geometric shapes are the triangle, the circle, and the square.*

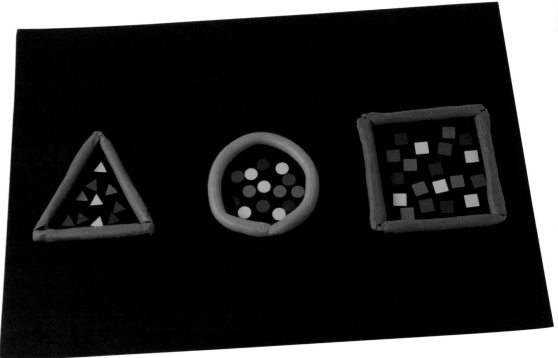

**TIP**
If you don't have stickers, you can use light colored crayons or paint to make shapes inside the clay outlines.

# Hands On!

*For this craft, you will explore symmetry and asymmetry.*

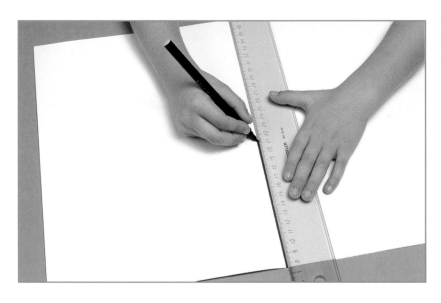

Fold the poster board in half, then unfold it. Draw a line along the entire fold using a pencil and ruler.

*The poster board is now divided into two symmetrical parts. One side is exactly the same size and shape as the other.*

Place one of your hands on the poster board, so that the middle finger is on the dividing line. Trace the outline of your hand with a black marker.

*Your hand is divided into two parts... but are they symmetrical? No! One side is not exactly the same as the other. They are asymmetrical.*

Use markers to decorate one part of the hand with little dots.

*And the other half?*

Use markers to fill the other part in with lines.

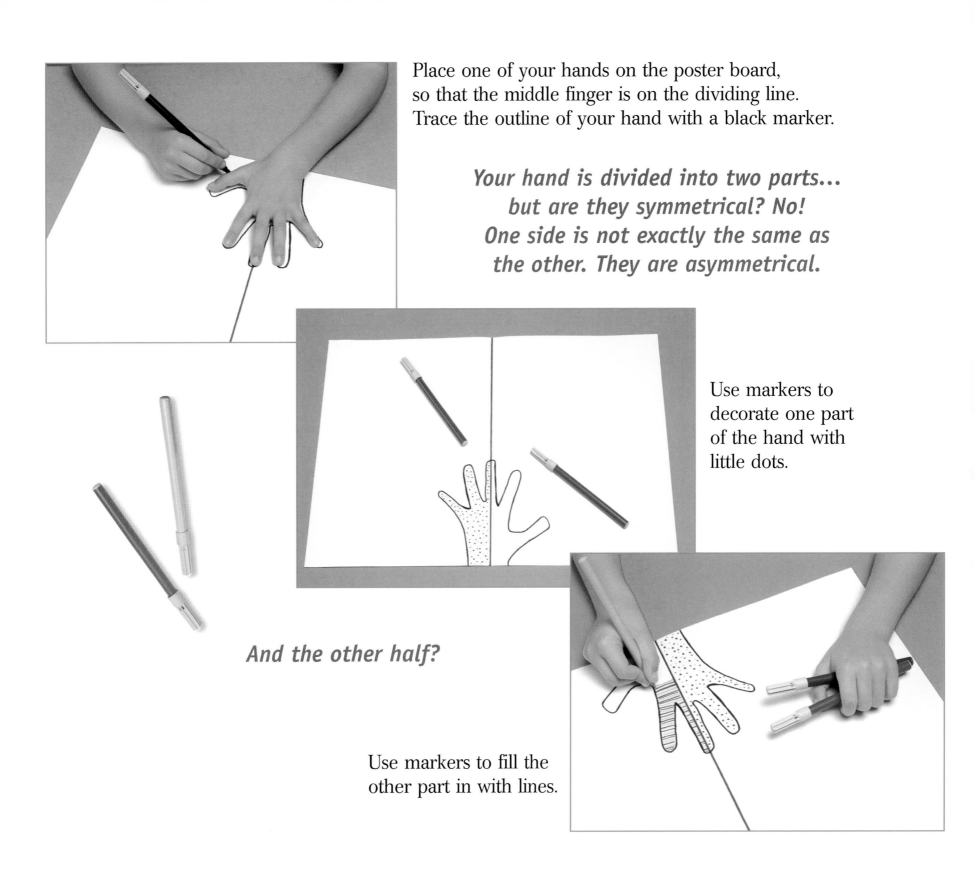

Put a latex glove on one hand, then dip it in red paint. Stamp it onto both sides of the poster board.

*How many hands do you think you can fit on the poster board?*

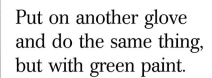

Put on another glove and do the same thing, but with green paint.

Put on another glove and dip it in yellow paint. Stamp it on the top part of the poster board along the fold line.

*This poster is a perfect mix of symmetry and asymmetry!*

**TIP**
Instead of using gloves and paint, you can use markers to trace around your hand, then color the hand shapes in.

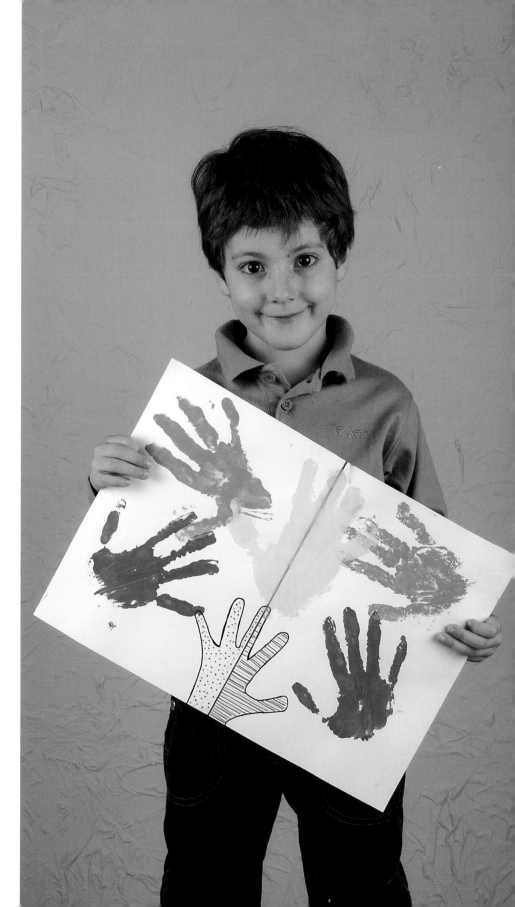

# The Ghost City

**What you will need...**
Two white poster boards
Black paint
A roller
Tracing paper
Magazine pages
Aluminum foil
Yellow clay
Glue stick
Scissors
Pencil
A paint container
Pattern (page 46)

*Have you ever looked at the outline of a city at night?*

Paint one white poster board with black paint. Let it dry.

Use the pattern (page 46) to trace the outline of a city onto the other white poster board.

Cut out the outline and glue it onto the black poster board.

**These buildings are missing doors and windows!**

To make windows, tear small pieces from the magazine pages. For doors, tear bigger pieces.

Glue on the doors and windows wherever you would like them to be.

With yellow clay, mold the shape of a crescent moon. Stick it onto the sky.

*And what shape should the stars have?*

Shape little balls of aluminum foil and glue them onto the black sky. Now you have stars!

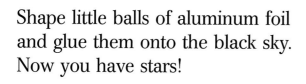

*At night, things take on
different shapes—just like
this ghostly city!*

**TIP**
Instead of clay and foil, you can use yellow
and light blue construction paper.

# Imitations

## What you will need...
Three different rocks
Clay
Wooden board
White glue
Dirt
Grass

*For this craft you will need three rocks with different shapes, a little bit of dirt, and some grass.*

Spread white glue all over the wooden board. Carefully stick on the dirt and grass.

Place your three rocks on the board.

**Look at the three rocks closely.
Do they have different outlines?**

Mold pieces of clay to make them look like the shape of each rock.

Let the clay rocks dry. Place them next to the real rocks.

**How would you describe the shape of each rock?**

**YOU CAN TRY**

How would this craft be different if you used construction paper instead of clay? Could you still make the shapes of the three rocks?

# What a Sculpture!

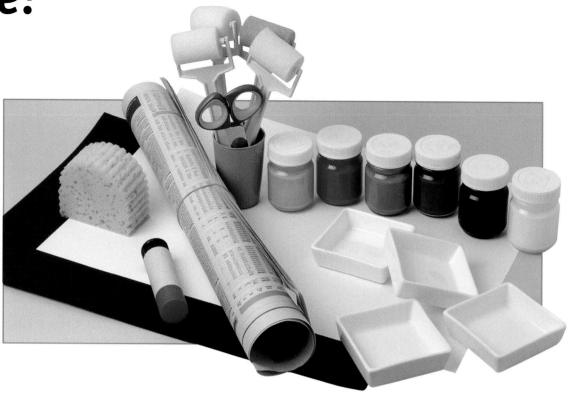

## What you will need...

Black and white poster boards
Pink, green, blue, orange, black,
  and white poster paints
Rollers
Sponge
Newspaper
Scissors
Glue stick
Paint containers

*Sculptures can have very original shapes. For this craft, you will make one out of strips of poster board.*

Cut the white poster board in eight long strips, each about the same width.

Cover your workspace with newspaper. Place the eight strips on top of the newspaper.

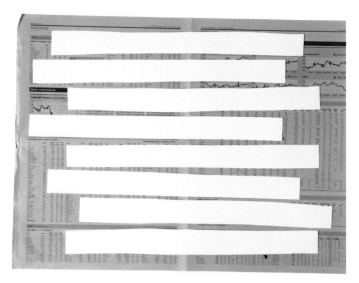

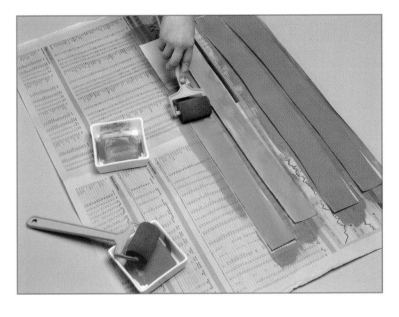

Get your rollers and paints ready! Paint two strips pink and two strips green.

**And what about the remaining strips?**

Paint two of them orange and the other two blue.

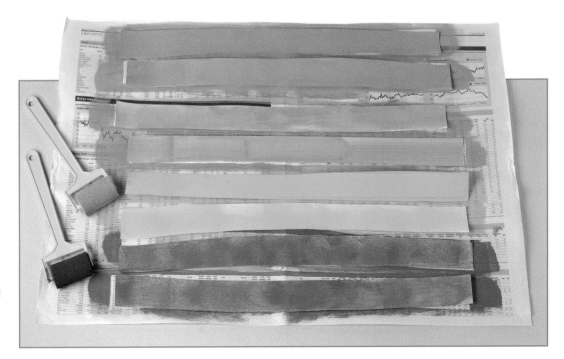

## Once the paint is dry, you'll be ready to decorate them!

Cut bits of sponge and dip them in white and black paint. Decorate the strips with small dots.

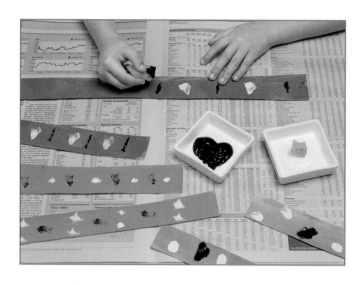

### Each small dot has a different shape!

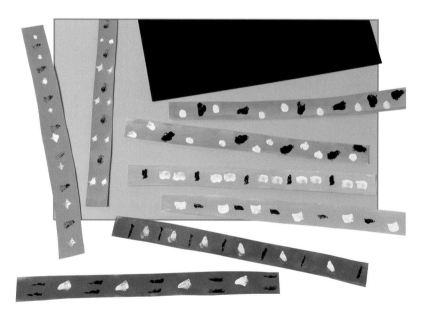

Wait for the strips to dry, then get the black poster board. This will be the base of the sculpture.

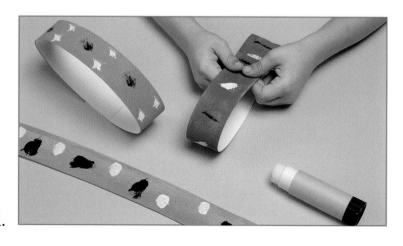

Spread a little glue on the end of each strip and start sticking them together in different ways. Then glue them to the black poster board.

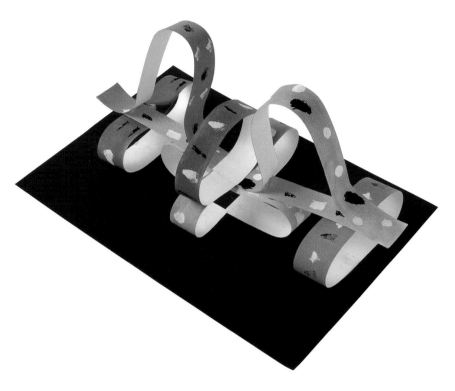

*You can make any shapes you like.
Now that is a crazy sculpture!*

**YOU CAN TRY**

Try making another shape sculpture. This time,
cut different shapes out of paper instead of
cutting the paper into strips. How does it
compare to your first sculpture?

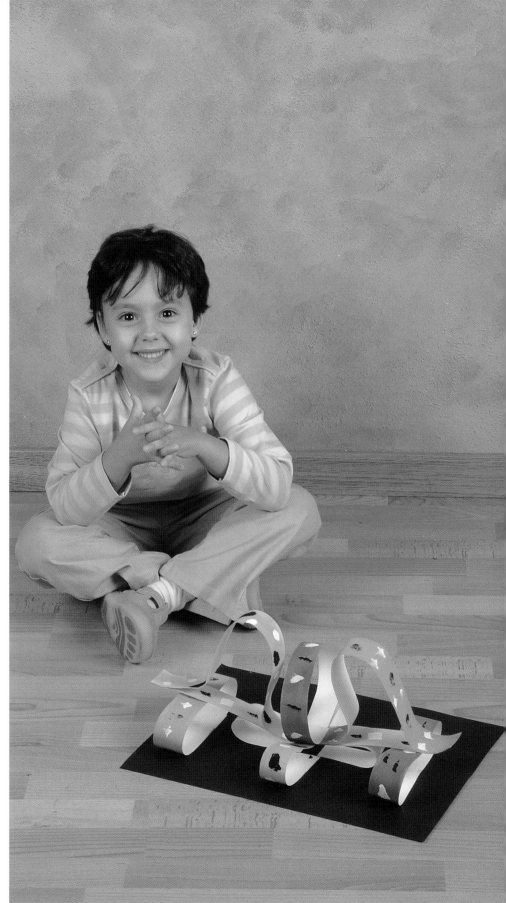

# The Super Spot

## What you will need...

White poster board
Black marker
Blue, pink, white, yellow, and red poster paints
Paintbrush

*All you need for this craft is a sheet of poster board and different colored paints...*

Fold the white poster board in half. Draw a line along the fold with a black marker.

Put a little blue paint on the center of the black line. Put a little pink paint above and below the blue spot.

Put white paint on the blue spot. Put dots of yellow and red paint on one half of the poster board.

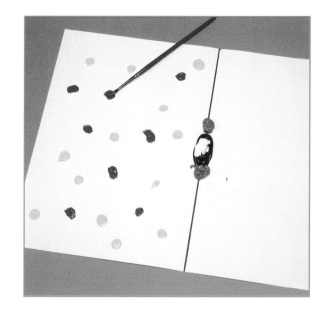

Carefully fold the poster board again, the same way as before. Press it down to make sure the paint spreads.

*Open the poster board. Surprise! The paint has made a symmetrical shape. This one looks a little like a crazy bug. What does yours look like?*

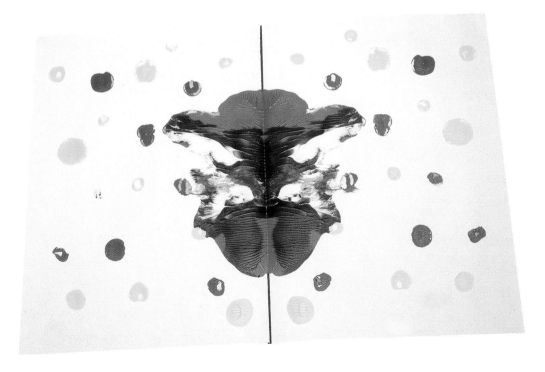

**YOU CAN TRY**
What other symmetrical shapes can you make? Try putting the paint on in different ways and see how it turns out.

# The Architect

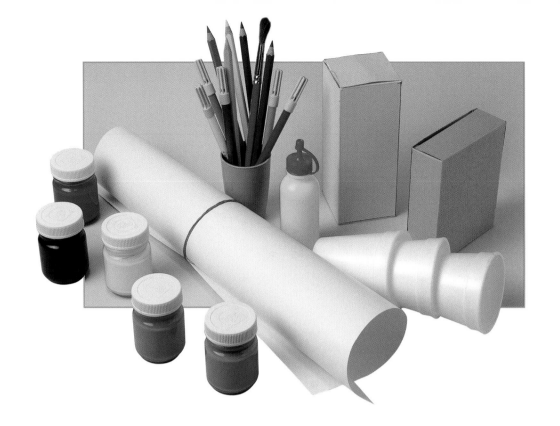

## What you will need...

White poster board
Colored pencils
Markers (different colors)
Two cardboard boxes (different sizes)
Three foam cups
Red, orange, green, dark blue, and yellow poster paint
White glue
Paintbrushes

*To be an architect, you have to know how to draw good building plans.*
*First you have to decide what shapes you are going to build!*

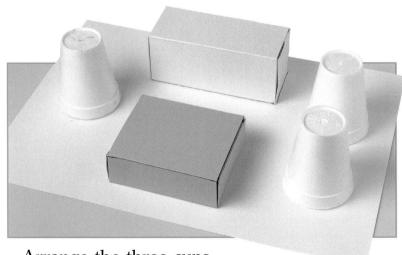

Arrange the three cups
and the two boxes on the
white poster board.

With a marker, trace the outline of one box.

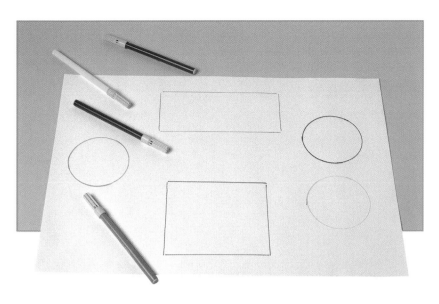

Using a different color each time, trace the outlines of the other cups and boxes. Then remove the objects.

*You still have the same shapes, but they are flat!*

Paint the cups and boxes different colors.

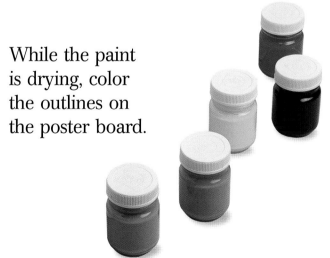

While the paint is drying, color the outlines on the poster board.

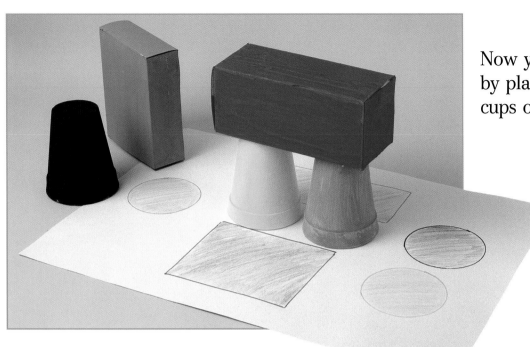

Now you can build a tower by placing the boxes and cups on the poster board.

**_Doesn't your building need cement to hold it together?_**

When you like the shape of your tower, glue the boxes and cups together with white glue.

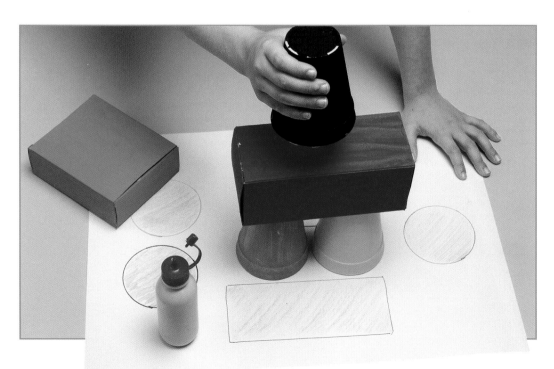

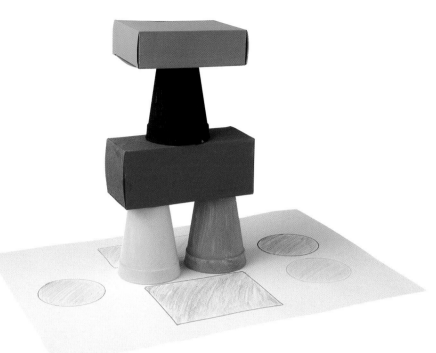

*You have gone from a drawing on a flat surface to a three-dimensional tower. What a great architect!*

**YOU CAN TRY**
What kind of tower can you build using other materials? Try adding in an empty coffee can, a paper towel tube, a shoe box...how big can your tower get?

# Autumn Shapes

*Many leaves fall in autumn.
Do you know their shapes?*

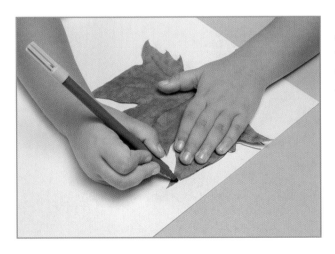

Place a leaf on one of the lower corners of the poster board. Trace the outline with a green marker.

Now place the leaf in the opposite corner of the poster board. Trace it with a red marker.

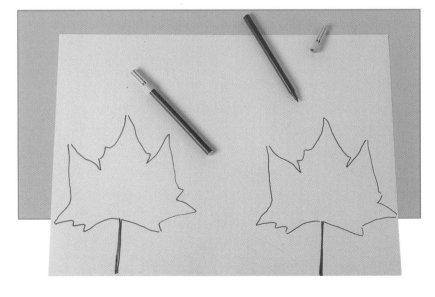

**Now you have two empty shapes.
Do you want to fill one in?**

Make little balls of colored
tissue paper. Glue them
inside the green leaf.

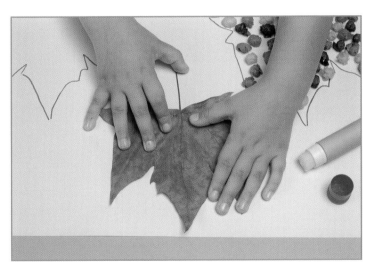

Glue the real leaf to the top
section of the poster board.

**Which of the three shapes
do you like the most?**

**TIP**
If you don't have tissue paper, you can use
crayons or markers to fill in the leaf.

# Building on Shapes

## What you will need...

Pink poster board
Black marker
Glue stick
Tissue paper (different colors)
Two yellow buttons
Blue shoelace
Newspaper
Toothpicks

*Can you imagine all the shapes that can be made from a triangle, a square, and a circle?*

Draw an upside-down triangle, a square, and a circle on the poster board.

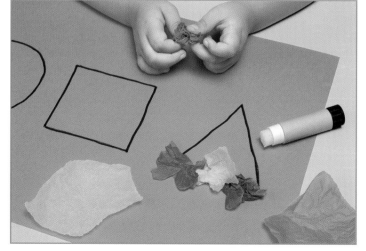

Crumple up the tissue paper and glue the pieces to the base of the triangle.

*Does it remind you of an ice cream cone?*

Now glue two buttons inside the circle, like eyes. Glue a piece of string for the mouth and other pieces for the hair.

*Doesn't it look like a face?*

Tear a piece of newspaper in a triangle shape and glue it onto the square for a roof. Glue three toothpicks in the square to make a door. Now you have a house!

*Do you see how easy it is to transform the three basic shapes into other things?*

**YOU CAN TRY**
What other things can you make with simple shapes?

# A Symmetrical Flower

## What you will need...
White poster board
4 green leaves
Blue marker
Orange, red, and blue cellophane
Tracing paper
Scissors
Hole puncher or scissors
Glue stick
Ruler
Pencil
Pattern (page 47)

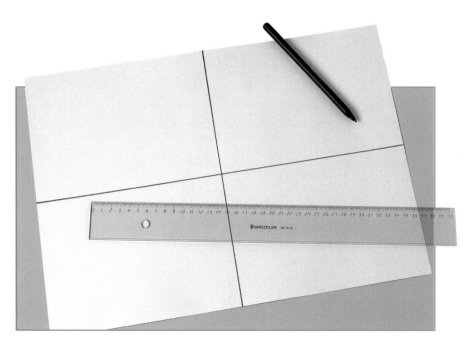

*Do you know that you can have vertical symmetry as well as horizontal symmetry?*

With a ruler and a black marker, draw a vertical line and a horizontal line on the poster board to divide it into four equal parts.

Use the pattern (page 47) to trace the shape of a flower onto the poster board. The lines of the petals and the middle of the flower should line up with the lines on the poster board.

*Now you have the flower centered.*

Punch or cut out the petals and then the center of the flower.

*We are going to decorate it symmetrically!*

Cut two pieces of orange cellophane, two pieces of blue, and one piece of red.

On the other side of the poster board, glue the two orange pieces of cellophane behind the two longer petals.

Now glue the two blue pieces behind the other two petals. Glue the red piece behind the center.

Turn the poster board back to the front again. Glue the four green leaves between the petals, so that they are also symmetrical.

*What an original flower.*
*Look at how symmetrical it is!*

**TIP**
If you don't have cellophane, you can use
construction paper.

# Shape Patterns

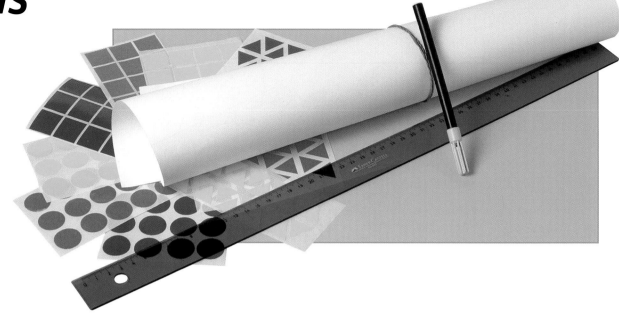

## What you will need...

White poster board
Large square, triangular, and round
  stickers (each in yellow, red, and blue)
Black marker
Ruler

*What kinds of patterns can you make with different shapes and colors?*

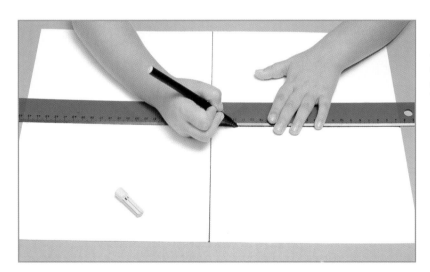

Divide the poster board
into four equal parts.

In the top left section, place a round
red sticker, a blue square sticker,
and a yellow triangle sticker.

## And in the other sections?

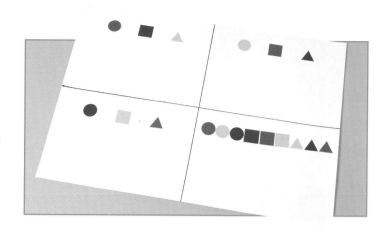

In the top right section, place a round yellow sticker, a red square sticker, and a blue triangle sticker. In the lower left section, put a blue circle, a yellow square, and a red triangle. And in the last section, place one sticker of each shape and color.

## Now you can start to make patterns!

Look at each section. Create new patterns using only the shapes and colors that are there.

## In the last part, you can make more complex patterns, because you can use stickers of all shapes and colors!

**TIP**
If you don't have stickers in all the right shapes and colors, you can use crayons or markers to draw the shapes instead.

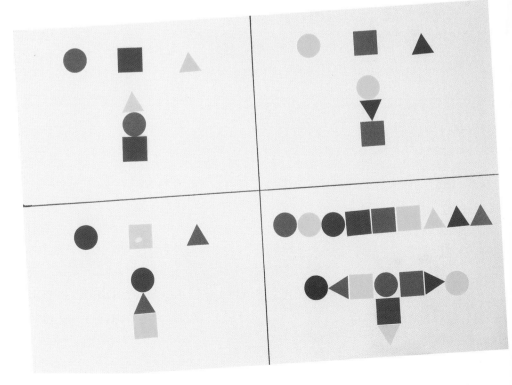

# A Magic Shape

**What you will need...**
White poster board
Hole puncher or scissors
Finger paints (different colors)
Pencil
Tracing paper
Glue stick
Pattern (page 48)

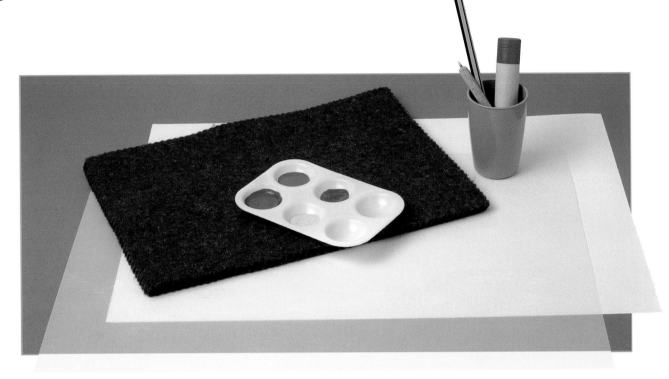

*Do you know that you can make a three-dimensional shape out of a flat one?*

In the center of the poster board, trace the shape from the pattern (page 48).

Punch or cut out this shape around its outline, but leave the bottom part uncut. Also cut out and remove the circular center.

*Wait for the paint to dry...*

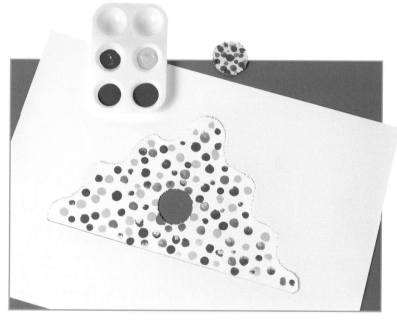

Decorate the inside of the shape and the circle with finger paints.

When the paint is dry, glue the circle below the shape.

Fold the shape up.

*Now you have made a two-dimensional shape three-dimensional!*

**YOU CAN TRY**
What other 2D shapes can you make into 3D shapes?

### "Woman and Bird" by Joan Miró (1892–1983)

Joan Miró was born in Barcelona, Spain. He experimented with many different kinds of art and had a style all his own.

His work features colorful pictures of abstract shapes, spectacular mosaics, and imaginative sculptures. For his *Woman and Bird* sculpture, Miró combined a large, long shape to represent the female body with a smaller, rounder shape to represent a bird.

Take some clay, then make different shapes and combine them. You can also make a surprising sculpture!

# *The Ghost City*

Pages 16–19

# A Symmetrical Flower

Pages 36–39

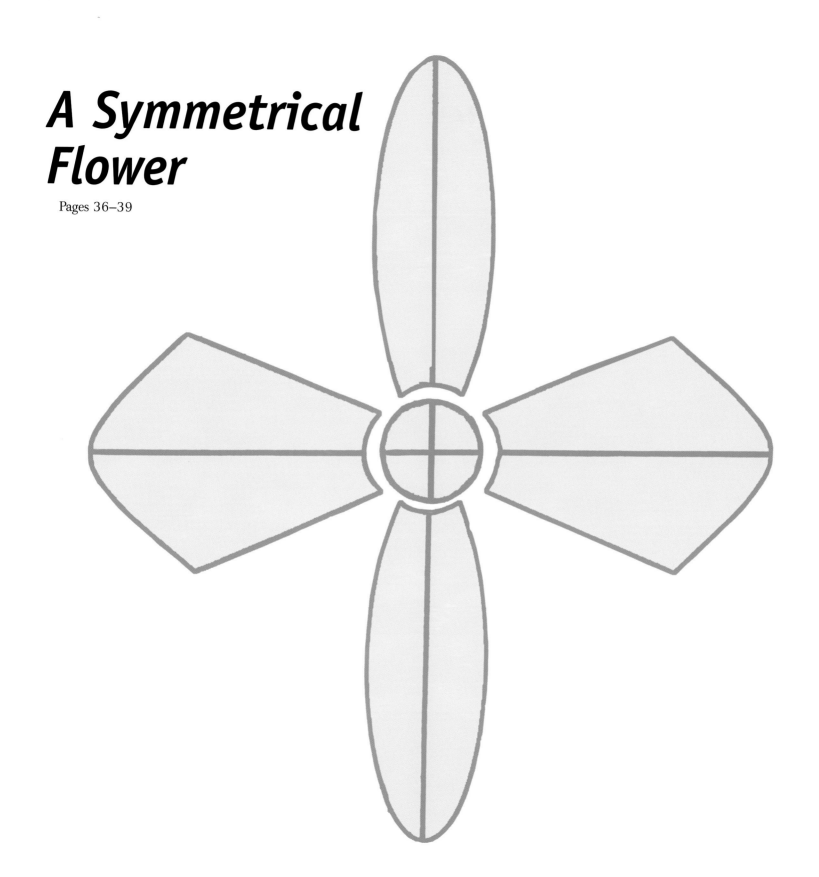

# A Magic Shape

Pages 42–44

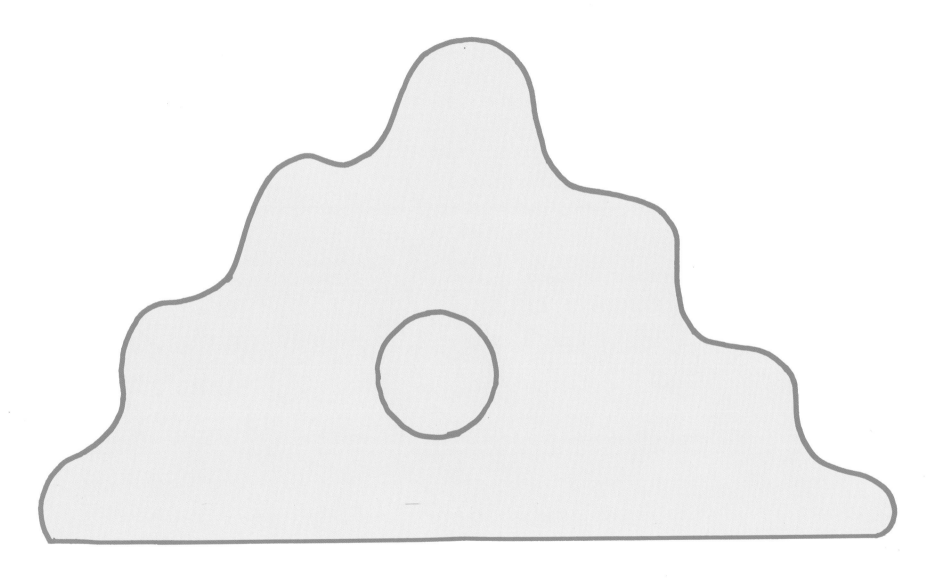